WHAT IF? WHAT ELSE? WHAT NOW?

WHAT IF? WHAT ELSE? WHAT NOW?

An Interactive Guide to
Reinvention and Living Forward

Sara Hopley Boatz

authorHOUSE®

AuthorHouse™
1663 Liberty Drive
Bloomington, IN 47403
www.authorhouse.com
Phone: 1-800-839-8640

Published by AuthorHouse   05/24/2012

ISBN: 978-1-4685-7261-2 (sc)
ISBN: 978-1-4772-0996-7 (e)

Library of Congress Control Number: 2012909370

This book is printed on acid-free paper.

To Ramon
Thanks for all the life lessons.
Believe!

Contents

What Is This Book?
What Is Living Forward?

Have you ever found yourself in a place where you know you *have* to make a change? Perhaps it is a life-altering event, or the people in your life change; maybe *you* change. It could be a milestone birthday or a life transition—leaving the workforce or returning to work. Your kids leave for college or a loved one passes away.

You may find yourself reflecting on all you have accomplished and dreaming of the many things you have yet to do. For many, it is the feeling of being stuck—soldiering through a routine to keep the bills paid, but little else—day after day, month after month, year after year.

Read the stories of others, who have experienced similar situations. Perhaps you can relate.

What if?

Jane celebrated her forty-ninth birthday on a progressive journey into her fiftieth year of existence. She took a long, hard look at herself and felt good about all she had accomplished. In the same breath, however, she found herself asking, "So, now what?"

She had met, or was on her way to meeting, all the goals she set for herself. What else was left? Was this as good as it gets? She thought she may be experiencing a mid-life crisis. She asked herself, "*Who am I now, and what do I want?*"

She knew there was more. This was her time for a reinvention. So she found herself asking, "What if?"

What else?

Brian had a horrible childhood of physical and mental abuse. His single mother did not give him the time of day; she told him he was, and would always be, worthless. He tried to do what he thought was right but did not really have a purpose or know how to set goals. He never had guidance.

He found himself waking up, going to work, coming home, and going to sleep, just to do it all over again the next day. Brian did not realize he was simply existing rather than living.

When this fact was finally pointed out to him, Brian knew he had to change; he needed a plan, a purpose. He needed to find a way to start living forward to figure out . . . What else?

What now?

After thirteen years of marriage, the relationship between Monica and her husband was extremely rocky; divorce seemed inevitable. Monica had been going through life, living day-to-day and in her heart, she knew this was coming. Now, it was here.

She had to make a change, no question about it, but a change to what? How would she change? She was not ready for this and was forced to ask herself, *what now?*

Not one of the aforementioned people was happy at this point in their lives. So I asked each of them: What if you changed your point-of-view? What if, instead of worrying about the past, or just focusing on existing in the present, you picked your head up and looked forward, lived forward? What does it look like? Surely, these are scary thoughts.

- To one, there appeared to be endless possibilities: What is right for me, now? What should, or *could*, I become?
- To another, there appeared to be chaos created by uncertainty.
- To yet another, it was too overwhelming to ever imagine anything at all.

The one thing they all had in common, they were stuck. None of them was living forward.

Living Forward is setting goals, having a plan, and/or taking action that enables you to engage in life mentally, physically, and socially. Really *live* life on your terms; the way you want; in a manner that makes you happy and engages you in the right situations, with the right people, and in the right places. Live to realize your dreams.

So how do you do it?

To live forward, you need to look forward. Taking steps toward living forward requires a little introspection, a little dreaming, and ideas and actions to propel you from where you currently are toward those dreams. You will need to inventory what you have to work with, what you may need to obtain, and identify the things that may get in your way.

Change is a process. And it is what you can expect from this book—change. By using the tools provided in the upcoming pages, you will paint a picture to help you not only set some goals for a better you and a better life but also help you become un-stuck and figure out: What if? What else? Or What now? This interactive guide will help you get focused on living forward.

Just remember, you cannot change the past. However, you can accept it and use your experience as the springboard toward a positive future.

Do not simply exist; live forward. Judge yourself not by who you were, but by who you are today and can be in the future.

An offer I hope you cannot refuse.

My challenge to you is to start on this journey today. See what it has to offer you. Use the tools in this book to help get you on the right path. If you want to talk about it, you can.

You have invested in this guide, and I want to invest in you. I am offering you a free one-on-one consultation session to review your work and tell you what I see from a professional strategists' perspective. I will help you clarify, prioritize, and focus on the right activities to live forward as fast and effectively as possible.

Please complete as much of this guide as you can so I can give you my best advice. However, if your guide is fairly complete, it may be all you will need.

If you choose to take advantage of my offer, the first session is free. If, however, you want additional time, we can negotiate an hourly fee for service to fit your budget. To set up your free session, e-mail me at sara@sarastrategies.com.

About the Author

Sara Boatz observes things others do not or cannot see. Her talent is examining relevant information to develop solutions that get her clients moving in a purposeful manner.

Sara turns everything on its side, looks at issues from every angle, and approaches client information without emotion. This objectivity allows her to develop creative solutions designed to meet specific client goals. She has been perfecting her craft for nearly thirty years.

The secret, she says, "It's all inside the client. I've just refined the process for getting it articulated, analyzed, and create the focus necessary to take action and achieve."

Over the years, Sara has developed and perfected the particular process you will find in this interactive guide. She has worked through it with dozens of companies, teams, and individuals to help them through growth and reinvention with excellent success.

Sara's clients have included small start-up companies, large Fortune 100 companies, and businesses of all sizes in between. She has also helped scores of individuals through this process, guiding them toward success to meet their personal goals. The process is the guide that will help you live forward.

Sara's work has been as a professional strategist—helping others plan a focused path. This guide will help develop, plan, and prioritize particular activities to move purposely toward your dreams. It works.

Sara tells those she works with, "Trust the process, but most of all, trust you. You have it in you. My process and coaching will help you move the right way to live forward."

If you want to stay in touch, you can do so through Sara's Living Forward blog. You are invited to share your story of total reinvention, or specific ideas that guided you on the path to living forward.

Visit http://www.sarastrategies.com, and then click *Blog*. Check in every now and again to read the stories of others, and possibly gain inspiration for your own journey.

Use the tools. Make some decisions. Share your experiences. Live forward.

PART I

What You Will Experience

The Framework

What you can expect in this living forward guide

The following is an overview of the nine-step process and the exercises you will complete to reinvent yourself. In a nutshell, you will articulate where you are today, and then dream about what you want to achieve in your lifetime.

We will work backward from those dreams, outlining what your life will look like three years from now. We will then set one-year milestones that should put you well on your way to meeting your goals.

At this point, we will identify every resource and strength you have working in your favor. These attributes are critical to overcoming barriers that stand between your current situation and the life you want to lead.

It is a lot of work, but you are worth it. Complete just one or a few exercises at a time; some of you will speed through it. Others will over-analyze each exercise and become exhausted. Trust your instincts. Write what comes to mind immediately.

Do some exercises, and then revisit earlier exercises to fill in information that came to you as you worked through other parts of this process. This will become a snapshot of you: who you are today and what you want to become. You will want to revisit this information often, celebrate accomplishments, and create your plan to continue moving forward.

One last note: you may be saying, "But I already know who I am and what I want." Good for you, then this will be easier.

Regardless, it is important for you to dump everything out of your head and onto paper. You will discover more than you know. If you feel comfortable, share your work with the important people in your life. It will give them a glimpse into who you are right now, and perhaps, they can assist in your journey.

The following is an overview of the steps in the *Living Forward* process:

Step 1: Who are you? Where do you stand today?

We start by painting a clear picture of who you currently are. Use the prompts in this section to describe exactly where you are, including the circumstances that caused you to arrive at this place.

- Explain why change is needed.
- Establish from where you are moving.

- Articulate who you are, what you do, what you are passionate about.
- Explain why it matters.

Step 2: Set lifetime goals.

What do you want out of life? Think *big*. What things will define you? What big things do you want to accomplish in your lifetime? These may include goals for your health, places you want to see, things you want to do, people/organizations you want to be associated with, or other material accomplishments you want to pass on to your children or someone special.

Some call this their bucket list. What do you want to be or have done during your lifetime?

Steps 3 and 4: In three years . . .

In these steps, you will work backward from your lifetime goals to construct an image of what you want your life to look like in three years. You will create a side-by-side comparison of where you are today, and where you want to be—what you want to achieve—three years from now.

Step 3 is specific about where you stand in important life categories. In Step 4, you will outline what you want your life to look like in these same categories. This exercise will help you create a list reflecting what you want to accomplish three years from now.

Step 5: Set one-year milestones.

In this step, you will narrow your focus to immediate requirements. What needs to be in place twelve months from now for you to be positioned to achieve your three-year goals? List milestones you must accomplish within one year.

Step 6: What you have to work with—your strengths.

In this step, you need to be a little more introspective. The exercise in this section will help you identify your personal skills and abilities. These attributes will help develop the strategies necessary to reach your three-year picture.

Step 7: What's in your way?

In this step, we need to articulate what is in the way of reaching your *three years from now* picture. Be honest. These barriers can be huge or small things. They could be habits you need to change, parting from people who slow you down, changing a work or personal situation you are in, or simply identifying things you cannot let go. What obstacles may keep you from moving toward your three-year vision?

Step 8: Assessment, strategies, and action.

This is the hard part. This is where you post all the work you have completed on a wall, stand back, and take a look. You are looking at who you are. What you want to be. What you want to do. What your life would ultimately look like. Everything is related.

We are going to take this information and use it to build a plan to start living forward. You will develop strategies, designed to use your strengths to go over, around, or through potential barriers to reach your one-year milestones. This will establish a path toward reaching your three-year picture. Exercises in this section will help develop short—and long-term strategies to reach your lifetime goals.

At this stage of your journey, I suggest you take advantage of my offer for a free one consultation session. I will assess your work, thus far, and help you develop purposeful and efficient strategies that will move you toward your three-year and ultimately lifetime goals.

Step 9: Revisit, celebrate, and revise.

After the first year, revisit your planning guide. You will be surprised at how much this process has focused you and how much you have accomplished. Take time to celebrate your achievements, big and small. Follow this entire process again, reset your action items, and your focus to continue to live forward.

How do you know you are living forward? If you agree with one or more of the following statements:

- This book and the tools associated with it have inspired me to take action.
- I have been inspired to set some new goals.
- This book has made me think differently.
- I have a focus and I am taking steps toward meeting my goals.
- I am working to establish or re-establish some positive habits.

This is an important point. It is not enough for you to go through these interactive exercises to place what is in your head onto paper. You have to look at it everyday and continue to work on it.

Revisit your goals. Realize some of your dreams and celebrate what you have achieved. This is a game-changer that works. It is you, not me, who creates the picture of the future you want.

You are simply going to use my proven process. Look inside yourself. Lean on your strengths and dream. Together, we will create the focus and strategies you need to live your life to its fullest.

I wish you the best and Godspeed on your journey. Onward!

One More Thing Before We Start

You need to go through this process with one thing in mind—think *stretch*. This process is very introspective. So much so, it can become uncomfortable.

At the beginning and throughout the process, you need to remember you need to stretch. Stretching yourself is not always comfortable, but it will help you reach higher.

I am going to push you to reach as high as you can. It begins today. I want you to do a quick exercise right now before you start anything.

Activity: Conduct the following exercise:

1. Find a roll of masking tape and tear off a three—to four-inch strip.
2. Write your name on this piece of tape.
3. Stand facing a wall—one you see every day. (It can be in your home, office, or anywhere in plain view during your Living Forward planning process.)
4. Put the tape in one hand.
5. Now, stretch with both hands raised, stand on your tip toes, and reach as high as you possibly can.
6. Place the tape on the wall to mark how high you are able to reach.
7. Look at this strip of tape every day. Remind yourself this is how high you can reach. Remind yourself you need to stretch your thinking throughout this planning process.

    Most importantly, remind yourself it is possible to stretch even higher. Yes, it may be a little uncomfortable, simple, and even silly. However, it will take you to new places.
8. Note: We will conclude this book with another exercise that involves this tape, so do not take it down. Please do not think about flipping to the end of this book to see the ending exercise. I realize this is what you may have been thinking. Trust me and leave it be for now.

PART II

The Process for Living Forward

Chapter 1

Stuck

People and companies get stuck all the time. Stuck is defined as caught or fixed, at a standstill, bereft of ideas, up against a brick wall. A person can get stuck on making a decision as simple as where to go for lunch. People can also be stuck in a bigger way. Such as being forced in some way to make a change—a spouse wants to end a marriage, an employer ends employment—there are endless possibilities.

What do you do? How do you get un-stuck? The answer: go back to the basics. Step back and take a good look at who you are. Define what drives you, what you are passionate about. This is the first step in figuring out where to go next.

With simple decisions, such as where to have lunch, the process is relatively simple. If you love Mexican food, the choice about where to eat narrows your possibilities. The choice becomes clearer; you get un-stuck, and move forward.

When facing larger decisions, however, you must articulate who you are and what drives you. Discovering and labeling these passions will help narrow your next steps.

Let's get started. Articulate who you are and where you stand today.

- If you feel stuck, articulate why.
- Paint a clear picture of you; what makes you, you.

Step 1: Who are you? Where do you stand today?

The first step in becoming un-stuck to begin living forward is what we in the communications industry call articulating the state of the brand. In this case, *you* are the brand.

First, I want you to write down where you are right now. How did you arrive at this place? Why do you need to make a change? Why may you need to think a little differently?

It is okay to vent here. This is an important step because once it is on paper you will be able to revisit the reasons you are doing this to remind yourself why you need to change.

This is where I stand today:

Activity: Describe where you are today—good and bad—including the circumstances that brought you to this place.

1

Notes

This is who I am:

_____

_____

_____

_____

_____

Activity: Complete the following statements as honestly as possible. They are designed to describe who you are. Write down why you do what you do. Reveal what you are passionate about. Be specific about what makes you unique. (Descriptive words are included at the bottom of this exercise that may help.)

- This is how I describe myself to others: _____

- These are my core values: _____

- These are the people, who matter most to me: _____

- This is what am I passionate about; what matters to me: _____

- This is how I take action: _____

- These are things I have accomplished and I am proud of: _____

- Other descriptors or indicators of what makes me, me: _____

Some descriptors to consider:

Introvert	Extrovert	Serious	Playful
Politically-correct	Honest	Risk-taker	Shopper
Thrifty	Emotional	Principled	Decision-maker
Frugal	Have a temper	Nosey	Love to share
Funny	Strong-willed	Wimpy	Influenced by . . .
Problem-solver	Good listener	Talkative	Hate change
Likable	Good at . . .	Not so good at . . .	Afraid of . . .

Notes

Chapter 2

Dream

Where do you want to go? It is time to identify your living forward goals.

In preparation for this next important step, you need to give yourself permission to dream and to do something about it. Some people find it difficult to dream about change. In today's fast-paced, get-it-done society, most people believe dreaming and dreamers are wasting time; not living in reality.

However, when I work with people who have truly succeeded in life; those who claim happiness, they consistently site allowing themselves to dream as a key reason. Make a commitment to yourself right now. Give yourself permission to dream; really put yourself out there and think about what could be, what you truly want.

When writing your dreams down—big and small—you begin the process of providing the focus you need to actually live forward and reach your goals. This is a very important concept. You need to tell yourself it is acceptable for you to dream.

Give yourself permission to meet some fun goals, scary goals, and goals you think are unattainable. They may appear unattainable today, but maybe not tomorrow. Let yourself go a little here.

Step 2: Dream.

Activity: Fill out The Dream Catcher

What are your dreams? Write down two or two hundred dreams—big and small—using the categories that follow. What is your bucket list? What are some things you have dreamed about achieving in your lifetime?

You do not have to fill out all of the boxes. You may have ten dreams in one section and one dream in another. These categories and prompts are outlined to help you begin thinking.

Of course, some dreams will fit two or more boxes; this is acceptable. Also, disregard the *Timing* columns at this point in the exercise. We will be addressing those later.

The following pages include two charts; the first is yours to complete. The second chart was completed by a client, who gave me permission to share her dreams and aspirations. Her responses may give you food for thought—idea starters to get your dreaming juices flowing.

Dare to dream big. And, include even your smallest dreams or goals; everything counts. Dream inside the box, dream outside the box—include things that may seem ridiculous, anything of interest to you.

Notes

Do not limit yourself. Even if what you dream is something you cannot fathom accomplishing, write it down. When your chart is complete, we will set priorities, and then strategize how to accomplish your goals.

For Monica, this exercise was difficult. Describing herself and writing it all down was not something she did every day. She found it easier to write some things down, walk away from it, come back, and continue writing.

During this exercise, she admitted she learned some interesting things about herself; patterns that helped her track her behavior. Some things made her laugh and ask, "Why on earth do I do that?" In the end, there were some behaviors she enjoyed describing, and there were others she realized needed to change.

While a divorce was a scary thought, sadly, Monica concluded her husband did not really fit into the life she wanted—she loved to travel, he loved to stay home and watch television. She loved to be around a lot of people, yet he avoided crowded places.

As hard as it was, she finally concluded divorce was probably a necessary change. It was very liberating. Rather than focus on the failure of her marriage, she was able to focus on her plans, which moved her toward the life she really wanted.

Embrace who you are. If you do not like some of what you see, maybe these behaviors deserve attention when you launch the planning section of this process. You are who you are because of the life you have lived, the experiences you have created, and the choices you have made. The plan you develop in chapter 8 will help you continue positive behaviors, build upon qualities to make you stronger, and reveal traits you may need to change.

If you feel comfortable, share your work with someone you care about, or whose opinion you respect. It will help them understand you better and, possibly, help them help you live your dreams. Sharing your work may enable your friend or loved one to be a better support for you as you live forward. However, this is certainly a process that can be followed individually if you prefer privacy.

Okay, it's time to do a little dreaming.

Notes

Activity: Use these categories to capture your ambitions. As an example, I have included Jane's dream catcher following the form you will fill out. Maybe it will spark some ideas.

Dreamer's Name: _____ **Starting Date:** _____

Appearance Dreams (How do you want to look to yourself and others?)	Timing	Relationship Dreams (With whom do you want to share experiences?)	Timing

Learning Dreams (Things you want to do or learn.)	Timing	Spiritual Dreams	Timing

Notes

Character Dreams (What you dream of being or becoming.)	Timing	Material Dreams (Things you want to possess or own.)	Timing

Work/Career Dreams	Timing	Financial Dreams (How much you want to earn or things you want to afford.)	Timing

Notes

Creativity Dreams (Things you may dream of creating/inventing.)	Timing	Fun & Adventure Dreams	Timing

Legacy Dreams (How or for what do you wish to be remembered?)	Timing

Notes

Consider this a work in progress. We will fill in the *Timing* columns after you have captured all your dreams. I urge you to keep these pages and add new thoughts or ambitions as they come to you. Check off the dreams you have achieved. Revisit these lists from time-to-time and celebrate some of the dreams you have attained. Re-focus on others you want to tackle next.

Example: Jane's Dream Catcher

Dreamer's Name: Jane _____ **Starting Date: October** _____

Appearance Dream	Timing	Relationship Dreams	Timing
Lose weight: 54 lbs.		Help kids and hubby pursue dreams	
Drink less alcohol		Solid relationship with husband	
Stay strong and fit		Be still and like it	
Have a face lift		Enjoy the day	
Have a smaller butt		Teach kids what is right and wrong	
Liposuction—gut, legs, buttocks		Stop judging self harshly	
Laugh more		Stop worrying about looking fat	
Maintain high energy level		Continue to positively impact my *third kid*	
		Believe in myself	

Learning Dreams	Timing	Spiritual Dreams	Timing
Experience new things		Figure out the Bible's relevance to me	
Learn by doing		Be known for something good	
Facilitate others to think differently		Change the way people think	
Live forward		Believe in myself	
Stay relevant		Be comfortable in my own skin	
Hear more, listen more			

Notes

Character Dream	Timing	Material Dreams	Timing
Be more empathetic		Get rid of old stuff I no longer wear	
Maintain my courage		Collect unique art for our home	
Demonstrate good character		Figure out what we need to retire	
Live out loud		Get a new car	
Be positive		Own an expensive watch	
Be funny		Have lots of cool eye glasses	
Be real			
Believe!			

Work/Career Dreams	Timing	Financial Dreams	Timing
Continue to make a noticeable and positive impact on companies, leaders, and teams		Be comfortable; able to pay for anything without worry	
Measure and celebrate impact		Create a financial plan for retirement	
Change how people achieve		Be able to live and travel well	
Write a book		Pay for kids' college tuition	
Become a paid speaker		Buy each kid a new car upon college graduation	

Notes

Creativity Dreams	Timing	Fun & Adventure Dreams	Timing
Write a book		Visit all seven continents	
Play the piano		Drink wine in Italy at sunset	
Lean how to paint		Cruise down the Thai coast	
Record a book		Go on a safari	
Speak to groups		Do a walk-about	
Make people laugh		Go to the top of the Eiffel Tower	
Write a memoir for my kids		Visit the Statue of Liberty	
Spread enthusiasm		Surprise and delight my kids	

Legacy Dreams	Timing
Raise the kids to have a healthy sense of self and independence	
Touch people's lives positively	
Have an impact on a lot of people	
Change people's point-of-view	
Be known for my energy, values, and impact	

Notes

Now, let's prioritize your dreams.

Activity: Set timing for your dreams.

Start at the beginning of the Dream Catcher; after each dream, complete the *when* portion of the exercise. In each *Timing* box, write a number to indicate realistically when you want to attain your particular dream.

- 0-1 indicates high priority or foundational dream you need or want to complete within one year.
- 2-3 indicates you hope to attain these dreams in the next three years.
- 4-10 indicates you want to attain these dreams after you reach your three-year dreams, and want to accomplish them within the next ten years.
- 10+ indicates these are longer-term dreams; ideas you do not want to lose, ones you definitely want to attain, but can wait several years.

Notes

Chapter 3

Your Workroom

A workroom is defined as a place to exert energy or effort to produce or accomplish something. It is a place where you surround yourself with all of the necessary tools and resources to get something done. Properly equipped, within this environment it is possible to ideate, plan, and execute change to create a new normal. It will be a very different place, a better place, than where you are today.

In this chapter of your journey, you will create a workroom. Provide yourself a place where you can house your work from start to finish—surround yourself with this work. This practice will enable you to develop strategies and action plans to meet the goals and dreams you have identified.

It can be any room that allows you to post your work on three of its four walls and leave it there while you go through this process. It can be your bedroom, office, or den; wherever you can come and go as you move through this book.

If you do not have access to such a room or need something more portable, buy a tri-fold poster board. They can be found at a crafts or drug store. These posters can easily be folded flat and put away when you are taking a break.

Or, if you are comfortable using your computer, create an electronic workroom, preferably laying out your material on one surface. This format can also be organized and stored.

Inside your workroom, surround yourself with strategically-placed information, so you can see everything in a glance. This will help to develop the strategies for living forward.

Begin by organizing information to paint a picture of your life as it stands now. This includes all the work you did in Step 1; put these notes on the wall on the left side of your workroom.

Next, take the information from your Dream Catcher in Step 2 about your desired goals and outcomes and put these notes on the far right side of the workroom. Now, we will work together to fill in the middle of this diagram with the steps, strategies, and methods by which you will reach those goals.

Now, make some category headers for your workroom. This action will help you organize the activities you will accomplish in the next sections of this book.

Notes

- Over your notes on the left side of the room (Wall 1), create a header that reads,

> **WHO I AM & WHERE I**
> **STAND TODAY**

- Next to WHO I AM on Wall 1, create a header that reads,

> **MY STRENGTHS**
> (What I have to work with)

- Next to MY STRENGTHS, as you move to Wall 2, on the left side, create a header that reads,

> **BARRIERS**
> (What is in the way?)

- Next to BARRIERS, on the right side of Wall 2, create a header that reads,

> **STRATEGIES & ACTIONS**

There should be a lot of space for the STRATEGIES & ACTIONS section as it has three parts.

- Now, we will move to Wall 3. On the far left side of this wall, create a header that reads,

> **ONE-YEAR MILESTONES**

- Just to the right of ONE-YEAR MILESTONES in the center of Wall 3, create a header that reads,

> **IN THREE YEARS**

- Finally, on the right side of Wall 3, create a header that reads,

> **LIFETIME GOALS**

Notes

Under this header, post your Dream Catcher pages.

Refer to the diagram below to see what your workroom should look like.

The Workroom

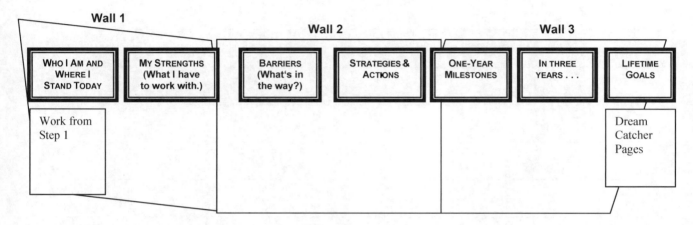

Your workroom is now ready to go. The information you have posted is the beginning of your strategy for living forward. Right now, you should have all your notes from chapter 1 under the first header on Wall 1, which reads Who I Am and Where I Stand Today, and on Wall 3, under Lifetime Goals, you should have posted all of those dreams you listed in chapter 2.

What about that gaping hole in the middle? Do not panic. The activities in the next few chapters will assist you in this discovery process. Your work, set up in this format, will answer the question most appropriate to you: What if? What else? Or What now?

Let's continue to move forward, so you can live forward.

Notes

Chapter 4

From Here to There

Steps 3 & 4: A picture of you now, and then in three years.

It is time to get more specific, so you can set three-year goals, get focused, and move forward. In these next exercises, you will describe where you are today in specific areas of your life, then outline where you want to be in three years.

Why three years?

Three years is not the immediate future, but close enough to clearly visualize. This allows you enough time to take the necessary actions to move where you want to go.

Can you change the time frame? Yes, you can change it to five years if you feel needed foundational work may take longer. Perhaps you are working with a key date or event, and need to shorten this window. Set your timeframe for eighteen months and get to work.

Planning can be done for any timeframe, as long as you base it on where you are today and where you want to be by the end of the allotted time. The key is focusing on short-term objectives that propel you toward your long-term or lifetime goals.

Various planning timeframes work for various clients.

One individual I worked with chose a five-year timeframe for her living forward guide. She had children in eighth and tenth grades, putting them on track to be out of the house and attending college in five years.

Her focus was two-fold: stay involved with her busy children and set goals for the nest becoming empty. She was preparing in advance for, "What now?"

A company I worked with used an eighteen-month planning period. Its internal mantra was *Speed is Life*. This was, and still is, a very fast moving innovation company dedicated to staying on the bleeding edge of the market.

For this particular business, industry conditions changed so fast, it simply could not plan farther out than eighteen months. This timeframe was successful because it immediately empowered employees and they quickly discovered new ways to stay relevant. Everything they did was based on, "What if?" and "What else?"

Most companies and individuals settle on the three-year timeframe. They find this allows for an ample planning period, as well as the ability to draw a roadmap for success.

Notes

Bob set his sights on his boss' job and used this planning guide to develop the activities and contacts he needed to accomplish his goal. Now, Bob is running his department with a new set of objectives for himself and his colleagues.

Activity: Describe where you want your life headed in the next three years (or in whatever timeframe best fits your situation). In Step 3, take a look back at the things you outlined in chapter 1, where you articulated who you are and where you are today. Use this information to help you fill out the left side of this grid.

On to Step 4—fill out the right side of the grid below. This work will help you set specific short-term goals in the next chapter. An example from Jane's living forward process follows.

Step 3: Today

Step 4: In three years . . .

Where I Am: What does my world look like today?

Where I Want to Be: What I want my world to look like in three years . . .

My Career:

- •
- •
- •
- •

My Career:

- •
- •
- •
- •

My Personal Life:

- •
- •
- •
- •

My Personal Life:

- •
- •
- •
- •

Perception: What do people think of me, now?

Perception: What do I want people to think of me in three years?

- •
- •
- •
- •

- •
- •
- •
- •

31

Notes

People: Who are the people are involved in my life today? Why?

-
-
-
-

-
-
-
-

People: Who are the people I want in my life? Why?

-
-
-
-

-
-
-
-

Skills and Abilities: Skills and abilities I have today.

-
-
-
-

-
-
-
-

Skills and Abilities: New skills and abilities I want to have in three years.

-
-
-
-

-
-
-
-

Notes

Example: The following is Jane's work on this step. (This may help you think of some items you could include.)

Step 3: Today

Where I Am: What does my world look like today?

My Career:

- Twelve years business ownership.
- Strategy on change
- Fast & efficient in my niche
- Slower than usual now
- Less stress
- Making big impacts on some companies and individuals

- Great experience with great clients
- Product launches
- Annual billing goal of $XXK
- My work is admired by some
- Playing with a blog & book idea
- Struggling with second business—trying to sell

My Personal Life:

- Married, two boys
- Very few close friends
- Two nice homes
- Good relationship with kids
- At home too much
- Unsure of value to husband
- Love being a mom

- New puppy
- In transition; at the end
- Overweight
- Physically-strong
- Making ends meet with less work hours
- Less stress, a little boring

Step 4: In Three Years . . .

Where I Want to Be: What I want my world to look like in three years . . .

My Career:

- Published book
- Guru status in my niche
- Sought-after
- Sales & Marketing Fusion work
- Second business sold
- Active blog

- Paid speaker
- Facilitate change
- Launch products
- Driving leaders, companies, and individuals to think differently
- Secure ongoing clients

My Personal Life:

- Trusted advisor to kids
- More vacations
- Trying new things
- More close friends
- Simplified life—not feeling pressure to produce as much
- More excitement and fun

- Strong and happy marriage
- Valued by husband
- Comfortable with weight
- In good shape
- Husband happier
- Have a retirement plan in place
- Low stress

Notes

Perception: What do people think of me, now?

- Smart
- Funny/witty
- Problem solver
- Successful
- Intimidating
- Misguided
- Generous
- Direct
- Quick
- Driven
- Scary
- Crazy for having people live in our home

Perception: What do I want people to think of me in three years?

- I make a difference
- Problem solver
- Good wife & mom
- Trusted friend
- Happy and fulfilled
- Admired for impacting people
- I drive change
- Good at what I do
- Solid morals & values
- Have the ability/ experience to help others move forward

People: Who are the people are in my life? Why?

- Husband & kids—Family
- Joe & Melissa—Like family; need better relationship with Melissa
- Anne, Sue, Bobbie, Carol, June + families—Closest girlfriends and family friends
- Sisters and mom—Family
- Jones, Smiths, and Barkleys—Long-time, long distance friends

People: Who are the people I want in my life? Why?

- Husband & kids
- More, new friends
- Anne, Sue, Bobbie, Carol, June + families
- More ongoing clients
- Sister in my city
- Joe closer than Texas
- Better relationship with Melissa
- Good relationships with long-time, long distance friends

Skills/Abilities: Skills and abilities I have today.

- Can see things others cannot
- Physically-strong
- Strategic planning
- Quick wit
- Ability to develop process
- I understand people
- Ability to manipulate
- Idea generation
- Creative problem solving
- Strategy and alignment
- Drive
- Teacher/mentor
- Good networker
- Ability to plan strategically
- Ability to motivate
- Shake things up
- Helpful to others

Skills/Abilities: New skills and abilities I want to have in three years.

- Patience
- Be a better writer
- More politically correct
- Clear process for Sales & Marketing Fusion
- Teacher/mentor
- Motivator
- Ability to enjoy the moment
- Filter between brain and mouth
- Know how to secure speaking opportunities
- Appropriate wit
- Game changer

Notes

Post your work in the workroom.

Take your completed chart from Step 3 and post it under WHO I AM AND WHERE I STAND TODAY. Take the chart labeled Step 4 and post it under IN THREE YEARS . . . Now, stand back and take a look. This represents where you are right now.

On the left is a clear picture of where you stand today. On the far right is a representation of what you want to achieve within your lifetime. In between the two is a huge gap. As we progress, our work together will help you fill in and close that gap—propelling you from where you are today to where you want to be in your dreams.

You can clearly see the beginning and the end. We will work backward from your lifetime goals to develop the plan to close this gap. The next step is to identify goals, three years from now, that will put you well on your way to meeting your lifetime goals.

Identifying your three-year goals is huge progress. This will help to define the types of people you want to be around, the skills and abilities you want to possess, and where you want to take your career or how you want to evolve your personal life.

The beauty of this side-by-side comparison format is you should be able to clearly see how wide a gap there is between the two scenarios in each category. The wider the gap, the more steps it may take to reach your goal. However, in some cases, there may not be a gap at all.

Example—Rick: When I worked with Rick on this process, he was very happy with where he was in his career and his skills and abilities. His gaps were wider when it came to his personal life, the people in his life, and the perception people had of him.

Rick realized he was focusing so much on his career he had let his relationships slip with his family and old friends. What he wanted was a well-rounded life, so his focus needed to shift from engaging in all work to some play.

This exercise showed Rick he needed to make changes at work to become more efficient, allowing extra time to focus on the important aspects of his life outside of the office. It was clear he needed to plan on having fun and re-establishing a few old relationships. Most importantly, Rick recognized the need to enjoy his family before his kids went off on their own.

Rick allowed me to share this portion of his planning process. It is clear that Rick's goals—and the method he used to articulate those goals—were very different from Jane's.

Regarding his job, Rick realized it was time to round out his life and take his foot off the gas pedal. He decided he could continue to progress at work, but at a slower pace for a period of time, so he could really enjoy his family and friends.

His children were in middle school and their high school years were right around the corner. Rick realized once the kids were grown, he could re-apply his efforts at work for further advancement. To maximize his family time, some of his three-year goals included:

Rick In Three Years . . .

- Working with staff to delegate and empower them to take over more of his work.
- Rarely, if ever, work on weekends.
- Have already taken one big family vacation and planning a second one.
- Able to attend every sporting event in which the kids participate.
- Re-established regular contact with three old friends from college.

Notes

For continuity sake, and to witness how this process builds with each step, I will continue to share Jane's work. She was ready for a career expansion, if not a reinvention.

Jane In Three Years . . .

- Get a book written and published.
- Meet and be regularly engaged with 2-3 new friends.
- Secure a minimum of two ongoing clients for Sales & Marketing Fusion projects.
- Identify and contract some appropriate speaking opportunities.
- Have a tested curriculum for workshops in place.
- Launch a developed plan to maintain the blog.
- Network to attract some new clients—fill the pipeline.
- Document (and potentially market) impacts in some way.
- Have already visited one new continent.

Hopefully, you can see in the cases of Jane and Rick, some big changes were on the horizon. For the first time in years, they were clear on where their energy needed to be expended.

This exercise shed light on the lives they really wanted and enabled them to move toward their three-year objectives. Jane and Rick ultimately felt empowered to develop the strategies and actions that would take them to the next level.

Activity: What goals will create your three-year picture? Look at your side-by-side comparison and outline what your life could or should look like three years from now.

In Three Years . . .

- _____
- _____
- _____
- _____
- _____
- _____
- _____
- _____
- _____

Post these goals in your workroom under In Three Years . . .

Notes

Chapter 5

Working Backward to Move Forward

Step 5: Set your one-year milestones.

Sometimes even goals set for three years seem daunting. This is where one-year milestones come into play. Smaller goals will help you focus on each step necessary to work toward your three-year goals. What do you need to accomplish in one year to be on track for reaching your longer-term objectives?

Wendy: One-year milestones were essential to get Wendy moving toward her three-year goals. Wendy had left a fast-paced career in the news business to raise her children. Now, nearly twenty years after quitting her job as a reporter, she watched her youngest child graduate from high school and head off to college.

She reflected on her years out of the workforce, and felt no regrets about her decision to be a stay-at-home mother. Now, however, she realized it was time to move on. As she drove away from dropping her last child off at college, Wendy looked out at the horizon and said to herself, *Now what?*

Wendy contacted me and we started working through the living forward process. She followed all the activities outlined in this book, thus far, and felt good about her lifetime and three-year dream scenarios. Ultimately, Wendy wanted to be back in the workforce, perhaps in the new and growing field of social media.

In her workroom, she took a good look at where she stood today. It was clear her twenty years at home left her far behind in technology. Wendy was not even sure where her skills and abilities would fit in a vastly changed market.

The living forward process helped Wendy define critical one-year milestones in her journey. It was obvious education, particularly in the field of technology, was a top priority. Wendy also realized meeting with a career counselor would help identify new fields of opportunity and the specific skills required for those careers.

As Wendy worked through the process, and made lists for her workroom walls, she realized certain things had changed. Describing her perfect world picture, she noticed very appealing types of work conditions. Equally important, she recognized there were other types of environments, especially those she once found exciting in the news business, that were no longer attractive.

Again, Wendy reviewed the lists posted in her workroom and made a commitment to some short-term goals. Computer education, networking opportunities, and involvement with civic groups became her one-year milestones. Although daunting, Wendy knew these immediate objectives, when accomplished, would set her on the path to her three-year goals and eventual success.

Notes

Example: Wendy's one-year milestones were, of course, created to get her on track to meet her three-year goals, which she identified as she went through this process. In her case, the one-year milestones included:

- Signing up and completing the correct courses to become up-to-date technologically.
- Identifying and attending networking groups regularly to gain a better perspective about local employment opportunities, and meet people, who may facilitate her goal of obtaining the best job.
- Performing a family financial analysis to help her identify the minimum amount of money needed to meet regular expenses, and save for whatever is necessary to meet three-year and lifetime goals.

Activity: To attain the picture you painted three years from now, write down what needs to be in place one year from now.

The Day I Will Begin to Take Action:
Action Date: _____

One Year from Action Date:
1st Deadline Date: _____

One-Year Milestones: (Things you must achieve in one year to be well on your way to meeting three-year and lifetime goals.)

- _____

- _____

- _____

- _____

- _____

- _____

- _____

- _____

To give you another example of one-year milestones, we will return to the work Jane has been doing. In chapter 4, Jane outlined her three-year goals. Working backward from those, what will she need to focus on this next year to get on track to reach those goals? Here are Jane's one-year milestones:

Notes

The Day I Will Begin to Take Action:
Action Date: **October of this year**

One Year from Action Date:
1st Deadline Date: **October of next year**

Jane's One-Year Milestones: (Objectives Jane must achieve in one year to be on her way to meeting thee-year and lifetime goals.)

- Create an initial bucket list
- Get the blog launched
- Lose 25-30 lbs.
- Understand family finances
- Set income goals for consulting biz
- Secure one new large, ongoing client

- Research publishing and develop a plan
- Research speaking opportunities and develop a plan
- Research good writing and employ practices
- Expose son to college soccer
- Bill $___K this year; take home $___K
- Have book outlined and started

Notes

Chapter 6

Work from a Position of Strength

Step 6: Your Strengths: What you have to work with to get you where you want to go.

I want you to drill down your introspection. What is at your core? What are your strengths and achievements? These are pieces of your value system and personality that will help you side step any barriers that may be in your way. Much of this work was completed back in Step 1, but it is important to revisit at this juncture—your strengths will help propel you into action.

Activity: Fill out the following chart and post it on Wall 1 under MY STRENGTHS.

My Values: (Core values that guide you.)   **My Passions:** (What is in your heart?)

-     •
-     •
-     •
-     •

Resources: (Skills, abilities, sources of income, and critical connections.)   **Accomplishments:** (Achievements to date.)

-     •
-     •
-     •
-     •

Notes

Currently Working On: (Projects already underway, but not completed.)

-
-
-
-

Strengths: (Personal strengths you have to lean on as you move forward.)

-
-
-
-

Sacred Cows: (What are considered must-haves?)

-
-
-
-

Other: (What else about you my help you live forward?)

-
-
-
-

Example: Following Jane through this process, she filled out this section as follows:

My Values: (Core values that guide you.)

- Honesty
- Do what I say I will do
- Creativity
- Drive toward impact

- Integrity
- Own my mistakes
- Doing what is right
- Half-full attitude

My Passions: (What is in your heart?)

- Problem solver
- Need to make an impact

- Love
- Creating positive change

Resources: (Skills, abilities, sources of income, and critical connections.)

- Good networker
- Know how to start a business
- Real Estate (Three properties)
- Network

- Husband's income
- Know how to run a business
- People I have helped

Accomplishments: (Achievements to date.)

- My blog ready to launch
- Good income last year

- The personal planning tool
- Board member of local community group

Notes

Currently Working On: (Projects underway, but not completed.)

- A blog
- Perfect smiles for boys
- A book
- Getting one potential new client under contract

Strengths: (Strengths you have to lean on as you move forward.)

- Physical strength
- Ability to review all angles of a situation
- Idea generator
- My drive
- Creativity
- Ability to solve problems
- My energy and drive

Sacred Cows: (What are considered must-haves?)

- My kids
- Husband

Other: (What else about you may help you live forward?)

- Goals from husband
- Framework for retirement

Notes

Chapter 7

What Is in the Way?

Step 7: Barriers—What may get in the way of you moving toward your three-year goals?

For this step, you need to identify any obstacles on your path to the *three years from now* picture, so you can devise an alternative route around these barriers. Be brutally honest; these barriers can be huge or small. They may be habits you need to change; parting from people who slow you down; or addressing an adverse physical or medical condition.

-
-
-
-
-
-

Example: Sometimes there are only a few barriers between where you are now and where you want to be. Barriers are real and have to be acknowledged, so you can plan accordingly.

Remember Brian from the beginning of this book? You know the guy, who had a broken childhood; simply existing each day? He was able to do a little dreaming and come up with a terrific *in three years . . .* scenario for himself.

He also noticed some pretty big gaps when reviewing his side-by-side comparison (steps 3 and 4) of where he stood today versus where he wanted to be in three years. From this work, his focus was clear: he needed to make significant changes if he wanted to stop existing and start living.

Brian was able to outline his goals and milestones, but had to insert a little reality by articulating what was in his way of reaching those goals. His barriers were simple and few, but suggestive. They included his inability to believe in himself (low self-esteem) and money. He barely made enough to meet his basic needs. This helped him realize part of his action plan needed to include activities to help him boost his self-esteem. He also acknowledged he would have to find a second job.

Notes

Jane's Example: These are barriers that Jane was attempting to overcome.

Barriers: (What things may get in the way of you moving toward that three-year picture?)

- A change in husband's job—less income
- Uncertainty of ability to attract solid, ongoing clients
- Perceived inability about how to write a book—scared of it
- The economy and fact I am a one-person company (less credibility to handle bigger projects)
- Low motivation and bad diet

All of these things had to be taken into account to effectively develop her action plan for living forward and meeting the goals she had set for her life.

Notes

Chapter 8

Strategies and Actions

Step 8: Creating the all-important action plan.

Sometimes people skip this step, which is like blowing off the maintenance portion of a diet program. You have done all the hard work to get here. Do not stop now. If you do, you will definitely stall your progress toward living forward. You can take a break, but be sure you complete this step.

Example—Gina: She is a client, who worked with me through this program. Well, most of it, anyway. Our session was—according to her—productive, exciting, and inspiring. She was genuinely stuck.

Through the living forward process, Gina learned she did not want to do anything involving her old career and skill set. She wanted something completely different.

Together we worked through the exercises and drilled into her dreams to determine what she really wanted at this point in her life. Gina was very motivated for the first time, in a long time. We strategized about her starting a small business in the area of her interest, but it would require some new skill development.

After hours of introspection, and many lists on the walls of her workroom, Gina had her one-year milestones established. Then it was time to create a strategic action plan: a commitment to the details necessary to move toward her one-year goals.

Gina realized these smaller steps would put her on the road to the three-year picture she had created. "Can't wait to get started," she said to me excitedly as she headed out the door for another appointment.

Three weeks later, we met for lunch. I was anxious to hear about Gina's progress. Unfortunately, the excitement and inspiration had worn off as life had gotten in her way. Gina returned to her plan, reviewed her work, and became reinvigorated. However, a key component was missing. Gina had not outlined her action steps and was confused about where she should start.

Sometimes change or a new direction seems like a mountain in front of you. What you need to do is look down. Focus on the few steps ahead of you—a few action items at a time—rather than the enormity of the task. Little-by-little, you will reach the top of that mountain.

A list of action items helps in several ways. If made thoughtfully, it will be your solid and specific path to growth. Listing your action items allows you to focus on one small goal at a time. As you complete each item, you can celebrate the accomplishment and cross it off the list—physically and emotionally.

Gina admitted she was overwhelmed by the many strategies before her and, quite possibly, a bit afraid. She did not know exactly where to start, so she did not do anything.

Notes

How do we accomplish this vital portion of the process? We break it down step-by-step, strategy-by-strategy. Here we go.

Take a seat in your workroom and take a good long look at all the great work you have done. This is a representation of who you want to be, what you want to do, and where you want to go. Everything is inter-connected.

In this step, you will use all of this information to build a life-changing plan to start living forward. These are the steps:

1. Look at your life goals; the big and small stuff you want to achieve (your bucket list.).
2. Now, focus on what you want to accomplish in three years versus where you are today.
3. Take a look at the one-year milestones to help you reach your three-year goals. You will use these to help you develop the strategies in this step.

Activity: Write each milestone in a box on the left column of the STRATEGIES & ACTIONS grid. Again, this step is where you capture ideas and action items for each milestone; it will help you hold yourself accountable.

If you want some help, you may want to show your work to someone you care about and whose opinion you respect. An outside perspective can prove to be very valuable.

If you are feeling really stuck on this step, consider taking advantage of my free consulting session you earned when you purchased this book. Contact me, Sara Boatz, at sara@sarastrategies.com to set up a time to review your work and brainstorm through this step of the process.

It is important to set deadlines in the form of due dates at the far right column. Make sure timing is realistic, taking into account commitments you already have in your daily life. These due dates will help you stay on track.

Notes

Short-Term Strategies and Action Plan

One-Year Milestone (What you need to achieve in one year?)	Strategies to Reach Milestone (How you will get it done.)	Actions to Take (Detailed, ordered steps.)	Due Date
•	• • •	• • • •	
•	• • •	• • • •	
•	• • •	• • • •	
•	• • •	• • • •	

Notes

One-Year Milestone (What you need to achieve in one year?)	Strategies to Reach Milestone (How you will get it done.)	Actions to Take (Detailed, ordered steps.)	Due Date
•	• • •	• • • •	
•	• • •	• • • •	
•	• • •	• • • •	
•	• • •	• • • •	

Notes

Example: Completing Jane's process, the following chart details her plan:

One-Year Milestone (What you need to achieve in one year.)	Strategies to Reach Milestone (How you will get it done.)	Actions to Take (Detailed, ordered steps.)	Due Date
• Lose 25-30 lbs.	• Sign up at Weight Watchers® • Stick to it for fifteen weeks • Celebrate success along the way	• Count points • Weigh in weekly • Read all literature • Exercise three days/week	NOW; early August
• Understand finances	• Meet with husband to develop outline • Set retirement goals	• Meetings with husband	End of June
• Set three-year income goals for consulting biz	• Understand financial plan • Plan for alternate scenarios	• Review financials • Develop Plan B	Summer
• Secure one new, large client	• Keep working with potential new client • Network to connect with other potentials	• Close planning meeting project • Meet with potential new client • Outline what can be done • Attend local networking functions	June
• Have book outlined and started	• Look for someone to help/edit • Develop some draft pages	• Start writing • Meet with editor in the fall	End of Year

Notes

One-Year Milestone (What you need to achieve in one year.)	Strategies to Reach Milestone (How you will get it done.)	Actions to Take (Detailed, ordered steps.)	Due Date
• Bill $___K this year, take home $__K	• Review expenses to be sure $__K is possible with a $___K gross • Keep working potential client • Networking	• Review expenses • Close planning meeting project • Regular meetings with potential client	June May June
• Research publishing	• Internet research • Primary research	• Online research • Talk to people	Fall

Notes

Chapter 9

Celebrate, Revisit, Revise

You are done; at least, with the initial plan, anyway. Congratulations! You probably agree it was a lot of hard work. You should celebrate. Actually, you should celebrate with every accomplishment, no matter how big or small. What you are looking for is *progress* not perfection.

Celebrating your wins along the way is just as important as creating the plan to achieve each success. It is important because each accomplishment will make you feel good about yourself. This acknowledgement of progress will keep you focused on the steps still needed to reach bigger goals and dreams.

After the first year, revisit your planning guide. You will be surprised at how much this process has focused you and what you have accomplished. Take time to celebrate your achievements: big and small. Follow this entire process again, reset your action items, and focus to continue to live forward.

Activity: Get your calendar. Turn to the page or screen, which displays the one-year anniversary of the start of this journey. Write in the calendar to revisit your plan when you reach this one-year benchmark.

Celebrate everything you have accomplished. Notice action items not completed. If they are still relevant, set a new deadline to re-focus you on getting them accomplished.

Some items in your plan may have changed. Maybe you lost interest in something or decided it was not the right time to pursue. Life changes and can often surprise us. After one year, it is time to revise your plan. Start at the beginning by reviewing your goals. Make changes, form new lists, and update your ambitions.

Do not be discouraged if you were unable to achieve some of your goals. Instead, celebrate your successes to date. If you have new dreams, add them to your Dream Catcher. These new dreams will require you to revamp your IN THREE YEARS . . . section. Simply push your new objectives out one year.

Of course, you will have to establish new one-year milestones, and create new strategies and actions to attain them. As stated, everything builds on all you have accomplished in the past and things you want to do in the future.

How do you know you are living forward? If you agree with one or more of the following statements:

- This book and the tools associated with it have inspired me to take action.
- I have been inspired to set some new goals.
- This book has made me think differently.
- I have a focus and I am taking steps toward meeting my goals.
- I am working to establish or re-establish some positive habits.

Notes

One Last Thing . . .

You Can Inspire You

Remember the exercise at the beginning of this book? The one where you were asked to think, *Stretch*? If you participated, you still have a piece of tape somewhere on your wall. This tape marked the highest point on the wall you could reach before starting this living forward planning journey.

It is time to stretch again. Think about where this journey has taken you. You should feel a sense of excitement about the focus you have created, knowing exactly which steps you have already taken and others you need to take to continue living forward. Here is what you need to do:

Activity: Conduct the following exercise:

1. Stand facing the wall where you placed the tape in the very first exercise.
2. Now, stretch with both hands raised, stand on your tip toes, and reach as high as you possibly can.
3. Did you reach the tape? Did you reach higher than the tape? By a little, or a lot?

After going through a planning process such as this living forward planning guide, most people are able to reach higher than where the tape was placed when they started. Why? They are thinking differently—more focused, bigger.

Now you know what to do to answer, "What if? What else? or What now?" It is amazing how once your pathway is clear, you can actually reach higher: physically, mentally, and practically.

Keep focusing forward. Make the best out of any and all time you have left in your life. You have the plan. You have created the path. You know what steps to take. Review your work often.

Revisit, revise, and celebrate your accomplishments and most of all, enjoy being whatever you want to be and doing whatever you want to do. Remember, life is too short to not live it everyday, your way.

Keep moving . . . celebrating accomplishments . . . living forward!